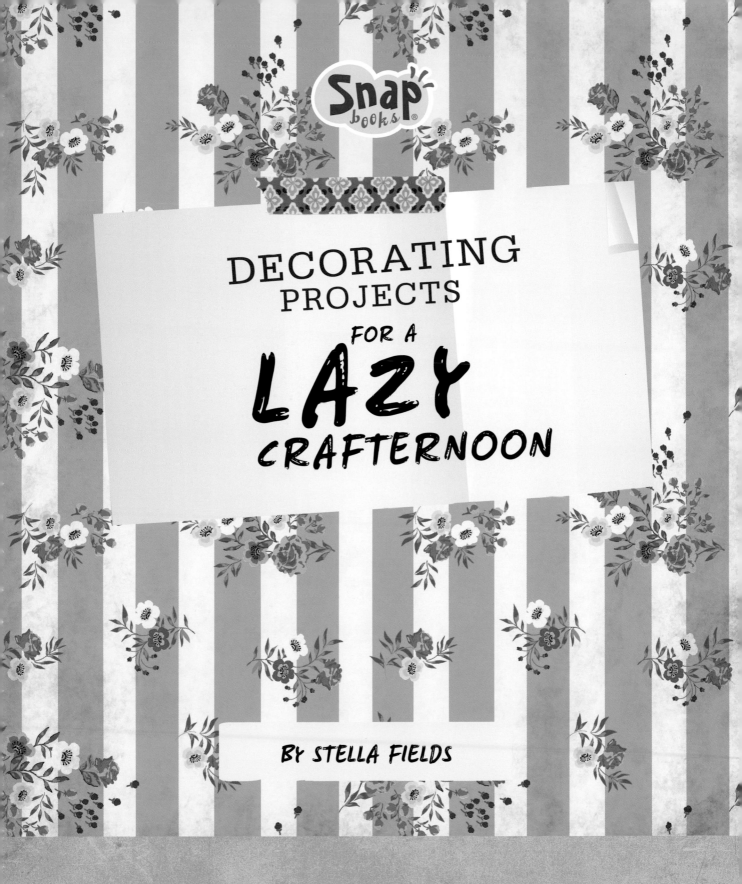

DECORATING PROJECTS
FOR A
LAZY
CRAFTERNOON

BY STELLA FIELDS

CAPSTONE PRESS
a capstone imprint

Lazy Crafternoon and Snap are published by
Capstone Press
A Capstone imprint
1710 Roe Crest Drive
North Mankato, Minnesota 56003
www.mycapstone.com

Library of Congress Cataloging-in-Publication Data is available on the
Library of Congress website.

ISBN: 978-1-5157-1435-4

Summary: Use this craft book to spend a lazy crafternoon making
decorating projects with your friends.

Designer: Lori Bye
Creative Director: Heather Kindseth
Photos: Karon Dubke/Capstone Studio

Projects crafted by Lori Blackwell, Mari Bolte, Lori Bye,
Sarah Holden, Heather Kindseth, Marcy Morin, Sarah Schuette

Image credits: Shutterstock: Africa Studio, back cover (right), Ann Haritonenko, 5 (top right),
nenetus, 5 (top left), Pressmaster, 5 (bottom)

Design Elements: Shutterstock: luanateutzi, pixelliebe, Studio Lulu, Tossaporn Sakkabanchom

Special thanks to Dede Barton, Shelly Lyons, and Mari Bolte

Printed and bound in the USA.
009687F16

CONTENTS

LAZY CRAFTERNOON

A lazy crafternoon is a day you spend with your friends, each of you making something incredible. Doesn't sound lazy, right? But it can feel like it, especially with the fun, pretty projects in this book.

These projects can be done on your own — nothing requires more than one person — but it's always more fun to spend a lazy crafternoon making things with your friends. The crafts in this book are great for beginners, but they can be taken to a new level by crafters with more experience. Invite girls who already craft on their own, but don't stop there. Your fashionista friend already has a great sense for fabric. Your musician friend knows how to put things together. Your movie-loving friend has an eye for what looks great.

You'll need plenty of supplies. You can choose projects from this book and stock the supplies yourself, or just ask your friends to bring what they have. Many of the projects here use things you already have around the house.

Before your friends arrive, get everything set up in your crafting space. You can craft on your bedroom floor or outside, but you might want to find a table where you can lay out the supplies and have room for everyone to work.

Snacks on sticks or cut into small, bite-sized pieces are great choices for people who don't want to get their hands dirty mid-craft. Check out page 28 for a perfect drink to serve your friends.

That's it! Now get lazy.

SUPPLIES

acrylic sealer
adhesive letters
black fabric marker
canvas
chalk
chalkboard paint
circle punch
clay pot
craft knife
decoupage glue
fabric
fusible webbing tape

paintbrush
paint chips
painter's tape
pencil
permanent markers
ribbon
rotary cutter and mat
rubbing alcohol
sandpaper

glue
gold acrylic paint
gold paper
hot glue and hot glue gun
industrial-strength glue
iron
lampshade
large photo frame
light switch plate
mason jars and lids
paint

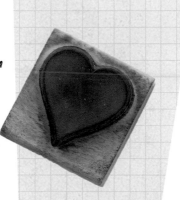

scissors
scrapbook paper
spray adhesive
stamp and stamp pad
stencil
straws
throw pillow
tulle
wire wreath frame
wood birdhouse
wooden shapes

NO-SEW PILLOWS

Get cozy with this easy-to-make pillow. Make one or make a bunch—the more the cuddlier.

1 Lay fabric flat, pattern side down, on your work surface. Set the pillow on top of the fabric. Trace around the pillow with the chalk, adding 2 inches (5 cm) on all sides.

2 Cut out the square. Repeat to make a second fabric square. Set the pillow aside.

3 Fold the edges of both fabric squares in about 1 inch (2.5 cm), and iron the creases flat.

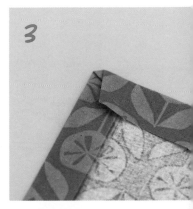

4 Place fusible webbing tape along the edges of one fabric square. Set the second fabric square on top of the first, pattern side up so the creases line up. Iron three of the squares' sides together.

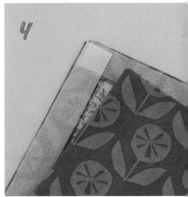

5 Push your pillow into the cover. Press the edge of the pillow down as you iron the last side closed.

Fusible webbing tape works like sewing without sewing—the iron bonds the tape to fabric. It's usually less than $5 for a roll that's about 30 feet (9 meters) long. You can also use it to hem too-long clothes or curtains.

This is a gorgeous way to add some color to your windows—or even a plain wall. You can draw a picture or create a pattern—whatever matches your decor.

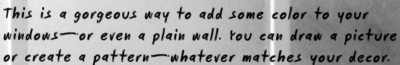

FAUX STAINED GLASS

WHAT YOU'LL NEED

large photo frame
rubbing alcohol
permanent markers
decoupage glue and brush
industrial-strength glue

1. Take the photo frame apart. Discard the backing and any paper inserts. Clean the frame's glass with rubbing alcohol, if necessary.

2. Decorate the window glass with permanent markers. Create your own design or trace a favorite design by placing it under the glass.

3. Cover the ink with a layer of decoupage glue. Let it dry completely, and then repeat, coloring each section again and making sure to add decoupage glue after each layer. The more layers of marker, the deeper the finished colors will be.

4. Outline the edges of your design with black or metallic markers to really make your design stand out.

5. Use industrial-strength glue to attach the glass to the photo frame.

Not feeling creative? You can use this technique to display a favorite quote or poem. Write the words in one color and draw around them in another, or write each word in a different color.

PERFECT LAMPSHADE

Upgrade a lampshade with fresh fabric!

Try matching your desk lamp to a larger floor lamp with the same fabric, or cover two same-sized lamps with coordinating fabrics for a richer look.

Make sure your fabric isn't too dark—paler colors let the light through better!

1 With the fabric pattern side down, trace the top and bottom of your lampshade, leaving 1 inch (2.5 cm) between the shade and the line. To do this, you will roll your shade across the fabric, tracing as you do so, until you have completed a full circle and you are back at the beginning.

2 Cut fabric along the line, then wrap around the shade to make sure it fits properly.

3 Glue the fabric at the seam on one side. Continue gluing around the entire shade.

4 Glue down the extra fabric on the bottom and top. If your shade has small metal parts, cut a small slit in the fabric so it can easily go over the metal.

5 Trim off the extra fabric on the inside of the shade, or add ribbon for a more finished interior look.

6 Add ribbon or trim to the outside of the shade for the finishing touches.

PRETTY LIGHT SWITCH

why should the rest of your room have all the fun?

WHAT YOU'LL NEED

scrapbook paper
light switch plate
craft knife
stamp and stamp pad (optional)
matte decoupage glue
paintbrush

1 Lay the scrapbook paper face down on your work surface. Trace the light switch plate onto the paper and cut out.

2 (Optional) Use the stamp and stamp pad to decorate the scrapbook paper. Work in small sections. Continue stamping until the entire paper is decorated.

3 Use the decoupage glue to attach the scrapbook paper to the light switch plate.

You can use the same technique with outlet covers. Of course, you'll need an adult to detach and reattach them; you don't want to mess with electricity!

PAPER SCRAP CANVAS

Get scrap happy! Put out a pile of paper for everyone to use. Then set up workstations with canvases and decoupage glue.

1. Cut scrapbook paper into 1- by 3-inch (2.5 by 7.5 cm) strips.

2. Arrange strips into a zigzag pattern on the canvas, plotting out the order from strip to strip. Leave a little white space between each strip. You'll have to trim some of your pieces to make them fit.

3. Apply decoupage glue on the back of each strip and place them on the canvas. It works best to start on one side and work your way to the other, making sure the space between each strip stays even.

4. When your pattern is complete, apply a layer of decoupage glue over the entire canvas. Let it dry, and then add another layer.

5. Wrap a ribbon around the canvas or paint the outside edges to give it a clean look.

You can use this same technique with fabric instead of scrapbook paper—or mix your media with both.

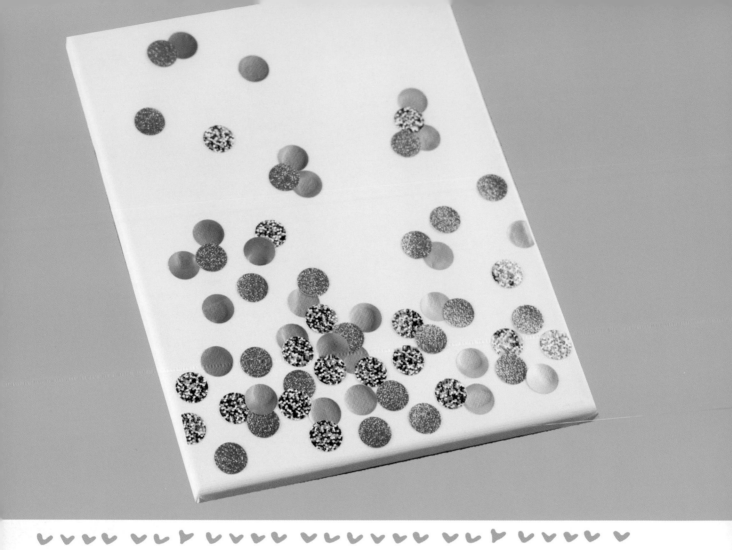

GOLD CONFETTI CANVAS

WHAT YOU'LL NEED

1-inch (2.5-cm) circle punch
two or three kinds of gold paper
canvas
spray adhesive or glue stick

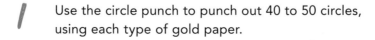

1   Use the circle punch to punch out 40 to 50 circles, using each type of gold paper.

2   Glue the circles onto the canvas in a scattered, free-form way.

MESSAGE CANVAS

1 Tape horizontal stripes across the entire canvas, leaving equal spaces between. Brush the edges of each piece of tape with white paint and let dry. Then paint over the entire canvas with your colored paint.

2 Allow paint to dry and remove tape slowly. Touch up any imperfections with colored paint and a small brush.

3 Once painted stripes are completely dry, lightly pencil a word or phrase on the canvas. Color in with black fabric marker.

Whether it's on your front door, bedroom door, or a wall, this wreath is bright and beautiful.

RIBBON WREATH

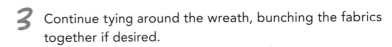

1 Use the rotary cutter to cut ribbon, fabric, and tulle into pieces about 8 inches (20 cm) long and 1 to 2 inches (2.5 to 5 cm) wide.

2 Start tying your pieces to the inside of the wreath frame. Begin with the innermost ring. Use a double knot to make sure the pieces stay on.

3 Continue tying around the wreath, bunching the fabrics together if desired.

4 Be sure to cover at least the inner and outer rings of the wreath. Depending how how thick you want your wreath, you may not want or need to use all the rings.

Use at least half a dozen different ribbons, fabric, and tulle for visual interest. Don't stop there, though. Use as many colors and patterns as you want.

You will need a lot of materials for your wreath. Buy more than you think you will need, so you don't come up short!

FLOWERPOTS THREE WAYS

Fresh flowers and growing green plants brighten anyone's day. Dress up simple flowerpots by using one (or all!) of these techniques.

DECOUPAGE FLOWERPOT

WHAT YOU'LL NEED

sandpaper
clay pot
outdoor acrylic paint and
    paintbrush (optional)
assortment of fabric scraps
scissors
outdoor decoupage glue
acrylic sealer

1. Use the sandpaper to make the surface of the pot rough. This helps paint and glue adhere.

2. Paint top rim of pot (inside and out), if you like.

3. While paint is drying, cut fabric into small shapes and strips.

4. Brush fabric pieces with decoupage glue and glue to the pot. Cover the pot with fabric pieces until all of the clay is covered and you are pleased with your fabric design.

5. Cover the pot with decoupage glue, letting it dry between coats. Once dry, cover with acrylic sealer.

23

GOLD PAINTED FLOWERPOT

1 Sand pot.

2 Paint the pot in a color of your choice.

3 Once the paint dries, tape off a section of the flowerpot with painter's tape. Use the gold acrylic paint inside the painter's tape lines. Remove the tape.

4 After paint has dried, cover pot with acrylic sealer.

CHALKBOARD FLOWERPOT

1 Sand pot.

2 Paint the rim of the pot in a solid color and allow to dry. You may need to apply a second coat depending on the color.

3 Use a stencil and small paintbrush to design a pattern on the rim of the pot. You can also leave the rim a solid color or freehand draw a pattern.

4 Turn the pot upside down and apply the chalkboard paint to the remainder of the pot.

5 Apply a second coat of chalkboard paint and allow to dry for 24 hours. Use chalk to write on the paint!

These sweet little houses look great together or by themselves.

BIRDHOUSES THREE WAYS

This craft is all about turning a zero into a hero!

PAINT CHIP BIRDHOUSE

WHAT YOU'LL NEED

acrylic paint
paintbrush
wood birdhouse
circle punch
paint chips
decoupage glue
craft knife

1. Paint the birdhouse and let it dry.

2. Use a circle craft punch to cut circles from paint chips.

3. Starting at the bottom of the birdhouse, brush a layer of decoupage glue onto the birdhouse. Position the paint chip circles on the glue, smoothing out from the center with your fingers. Alternate colors and tones on each row.

4. Apply more decoupage glue over the paper. Repeat for each section. Let dry. Trim the edges, if necessary.

5. To create scallops, let the circles hang halfway over the row below. Use a craft knife to cut out the shapes for the perches and holes.

DECOUPAGE BIRDHOUSE

1 Paint the edges of the birdhouse that won't be covered by papers.

2 Cut the scrapbook paper to fit each section.

3 Brush decoupage glue on one section of the birdhouse at a time. Position the scrapbook paper on the section, smoothing out from the center with your fingers. Apply more glue over the paper.

4 Repeat for each section. Let dry. Trim the edges, if necessary. Add your own paintings or drawings to personalize your paper selections!

WHAT YOU'LL NEED

acrylic paint
paintbrush
wood birdhouse
scrapbook paper
scissors
decoupage glue

FABRIC-COVERED BIRDHOUSE

1   Paint birdhouse roof a solid color.

2   Cut fabrics to fit each section of the birdhouse.

3   Brush decoupage glue on one section of the birdhouse at a time. Position the fabric on the section, smoothing out from the center with fingers. Apply more glue over the fabric.

4   Repeat step 3 for each section. Let dry.

5   Add ribbon trim along the edges.

6   Create roof adornments by covering wooden shapes with fabrics. Hot glue the shapes to the roof.

WHAT YOU'LL NEED

acrylic paint
paintbrush
wood birdhouse
fabric scraps
scissors
decoupage glue
ribbon
wooden shapes
hot glue and hot glue gun

SUN TEA JARS

Pretty and sweet, these drinks are a decoration and a treat.

You can use the decorated jars for other beverages, too—think flavored milks or fruit juice for brunch—but don't leave those drinks in the sun. Just keep them in the fridge.

1 Wash your jars before beginning.

2 Place fabric pattern side down on your work surface. Trace your jar's lid on it, and then draw another circle 1.5 inches (4 cm) larger on all sides.

3 Cut out the larger circle of fabric. Then make small cuts every half inch (1.2 cm) from the outer circle to the smaller circle.

4 Coat the lid with glue. Place fabric on the lid, pattern side out, and press it down smooth, removing all air bubbles. Pull the fabric over the sides and under the lid, wrapping them inside the lip of the lid. Cut off any extra fabric.

5 Use a ribbon to tie a straw to each jar. Add an adhesive letter to personalize each drink.

6 Fill jars with fresh fruit (such as citrus fruits, berries, or stone fruits like peaches or nectarines), a teabag (any flavor you like!) and fresh, cold water.

7 Serve tea with ice when you're ready to refresh your guests.

READ MORE

Bolte, Mari. *Eco Gifts: Upcycled Gifts You Can Make*. Make It, Gift It. North Mankato, Minn.: Capstone Press, 2016.

Kerr, Sophie. *A Kid's Guide to Sewing*. Lafayette, Calif.: C&T Publishing/ FunStitch Studio, 2013

Smith, Tana. *DIY Bedroom Décor*. Avon, Mass.: Adams Media, 2015

INTERNET SITES

FactHound offers a safe, fun way to find Internet sites related to this book. All of the sites on FactHound have been researched by our staff.

Here's all you do:
Visit www.facthound.com
Type in this code: 9781515714354

LOOK FOR ALL THE BOOKS IN THE SERIES